America's Supernatural Secrets™

Vampires in America

Sam Navarre

rosen publishing's
rosen central®

NEW YORK

Published in 2012 by The Rosen Publishing Group, Inc.
29 East 21st Street, New York, NY 10010

Copyright © 2012 by The Rosen Publishing Group, Inc.

First Edition

Library of Congress Cataloging-in-Publication Data

Navarre, Sam.
Vampires in America / Sam Navarre. — 1st ed.
    p. cm. — (America's supernatural secrets)
Includes bibliographical references (p.   ) and index.
ISBN 978-1-4488-5528-5 (library binding) —
ISBN 978-1-4488-5574-2 (pbk.) —
ISBN 978-1-4488-5575-9 (6-pack)
1. Vampires — United States — Juvenile literature. I. Title.
BF1556.N38 2012
398'.45–dc22

2011016361

Manufactured in the United States of America

CPSIA Compliance Information: Batch #W12YA: For further information, contact Rosen Publishing, New York, New York, at 1-800-237-9932.

Contents

Introduction

Bloodthirsty. Immortal. Irresistible. There are few legendary creatures as fearsome—and alluring—as the vampire.

But what exactly is a vampire? The question is harder to answer than you think. The traditional vampires of eastern European folklore were twisted, rotting corpses that rose from their graves each night to feed. These disgusting undead creatures preyed upon innocent people in their sleep, siphoning off the humans' blood and energy as they slumbered. Eventually, the vampire's victims would begin to waste away. Unless the vampire was located and destroyed, the victims would die.

The whole community would go to the graveyard and dig up the grave of someone who had recently passed away—perhaps the brother, sister, or child of an ill victim. If the body looked bloated with blood, if its cheeks were ruddy, if its lips were stained red, the corpse was considered a vampire. It had to be annihilated.

It was Bram Stoker's novel *Dracula* that introduced the world to the vampire we recognize from classic literature and old Hollywood films: an intellectual, even aristocratic, attractive, and genteel bloodsucker who seduced his victims and made them his slaves. He was forever evil and forever young.

The evolution of the vampire continues today. A new type of vampire has appeared in our popular culture: the glamorous loner, who may be more misunderstood than evil.

Why have our stories about vampires transformed so much over the centuries? Is there any truth to the legend of the vampire? Are all bloodsuckers from Transylvania, or can we find homegrown vampires in our own backyards?

Bela Lugosi's portrayal of Dracula in the classic 1931 film gave us our image of the vampire: tall, dark, and handsome, with a thick accent and a long black cape.

From the coasts of New England to the swamps of Louisiana to the dramatic deserts of the Southwest, the United States is home to its own terrifying tales of voracious vampires, revolting revenants, and bloodsucking beasts. This book's purpose is to uncover the hidden history of vampires in America.

chapter 1

Origins of the Vampire

one can say for certain when the first vampire story was told. But across the world, many cultures tell tales of undead or bloodthirsty creatures.

Vampires Around the World

According to Hindu mythology from India, vampirish demons called *rakshasas* and *hatu-dhanas* were said to live in cemeteries by day. By night, they roamed in search of babies and pregnant women to slay. According to Chinese folk-lore, a person who died through hanging, drowning, or suicide could return as a *jiang shi*. This vampirish creature literally hopped through the night, killing the living in order to suck their *qi*, or life force.

The ancestral homeland of our own vampire stories is the Balkans—the mysterious mountains of Romania, rugged Bulgaria, and the rocky Yugoslav peninsula. According to the region's legends, any person who committed sui-cide, died without receiving the Christian last rites, or died after a long, sinful life could become a vampire. These vampires were not glamorous: they were undead, twisted, rotting corpses whose hearts beat with fresh blood sucked from the living.

In Bosnian folk culture, when a mysterious epidemic began to kill off residents, the blame often fell on the first person to die. This unlucky soul was

India's folklore contains many fantastic creatures. Here, a rakshasa named Ravana, who is sometimes described as having ten heads, kidnaps the human woman Sita, an event that sparked a massive battle.

considered a *lampir*—a being returned from the grave to weaken and kill others, often its own family. Bulgaria was home to the *vampir*, a person whose burial was botched, trapping the individual between two worlds. The undead vampir might look perfectly healthy by day, but when the night fell, it hunted humans.

Transylvania, a beautiful, mountainous region in Romania, was home to the *strigoi mort*, a corpse who rose from the dirt at night and took on animal form. According to local legend, the creature would suck the life force from livestock or from its own family members. A strigoi mort could be laid to rest by exhuming (digging up) the body and burning it, or by burning the heart, among other methods.

Vlad the Impaler

The Balkans were home to a man famous in vampire lore: Vlad Tepes—literally, Vlad the Impaler. This ruthless leader's real name was Vlad III, but most Americans know him as Dracula.

Vlad III (1431–1476) was a prince of Wallachia, near Transylvania. During his lifetime, the Catholic West was constantly fighting the Muslim

A statue of Vlad Tepes stands in Targoviste Park in Romania. While regarded in the West as a bloodthirsty tyrant, in his native Romania he is seen as a strong leader who defended his homeland from invasion.

Ottoman Empire for control of eastern and southern Europe. Allegiances shifted overnight, and thrones changed hands frequently. Vlad himself held the throne of Wallachia three separate times.

The name "Dracula" literally means "son of the dragon." Vlad's father, who had once ruled Wallachia, was a member of an elite order of knights called the Order of the Dragon. Therefore, his father bore the Latin title Dracul, or Dragon.

As a child, Vlad watched *boyars* (nobles) topple his father from the throne. With the backing of the Ottoman Turks, the elder Vlad won his throne back but was forced to send his sons to Istanbul as hostages. Vlad's pursuit of the throne of Wallachia had more twists and turns than a mystery novel. But there was one constant: through his entire life, Vlad would seek

Native American Vampires

Before Europeans ever set foot on the North American continent, Native Americans told their own stories about supernatural bloodsuckers.

The Haida are among the many native peoples with stories about a man who discovers a monster feasting on human blood or brains. According to Haida folklore, the man tricks the monster and kills it, burning its body in a fire. But the monster swears that it will never stop eating human flesh—and the ashes that rise up from the beast's burning body become mosquitoes.

The *skadegamutc* is a supernatural ghost that is a part of Northeastern and Canadian native lore. It is a corpse by day, but at night its spirit roams free, feasting on human flesh and blood. In one tale told by the Maliseet people, the skadegamutc gains power by sucking human blood—and it can only be stopped if its corpse is thrown into the fire. It's no wonder that European vampire tales found fertile ground in the New World!

revenge against the Wallachian boyars, and against his childhood captors, the Turks.

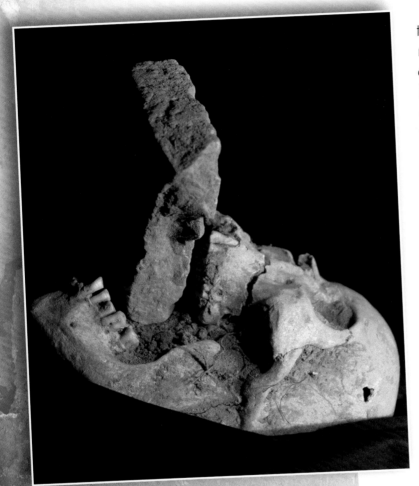

This skull of a sixteenth-century Venetian woman, discovered with a brick wedged into her jaw, is evidence of traditional European belief in vampires. People used the brick to slay the vampire and protect the living.

Once firmly on the throne, Vlad immediately moved to strengthen his grip on power. Legend says that he summoned his boyars to a grand Easter feast—and then had five hundred of them impaled. Vlad was known for a wide variety of cruel punishments, such as torturing, skinning, burning, or boiling his victims. However, he was particularly fond of impaling people on a high wooden stake and letting them die a slow, agonizing death.

According to legend, Vlad once held off a Turkish attack by creating a "Forest of the Impaled" at his border, half a mile (.8 kilometer) wide and 2 miles (3.2 km) long, where he impaled thousands of Turkish prisoners of war. The Turks turned back.

Countless scholars have considered Vlad III the inspiration for the literary Dracula. Bram Stoker is known to have researched

Wallachian and Transylvanian history. According to Stoker scholar Elizabeth Miller, he probably found the name Dracula in *An Account of the Principalities of Wallachia and Moldavia*. In Stoker's notes on the book, he incorrectly wrote that "Dracula" meant devil. (He was close: *dracul* does mean devil or demon in modern Romanian.)

Vampire Mania

From the late seventeenth century on, a vampire mania gradually swept Europe. The vampire superstitions in then-exotic eastern Europe filtered back to the West and caused a sensation, inspiring authors to write books and plays about vampires. In the Romantic Era of the nineteenth century—an era obsessed with superstitions, irrational emotions, and the supernatural—vampires captured the popular imagination.

When the colonies were established in America, vampires were already firmly rooted in European popular culture. The European settlers who spread across North America brought two types of vampire knowledge with them: images of the vampires they had seen onstage and read about in books, and the ancient folk beliefs of their ancestors, which they carried in their collective memory.

Chapter 2

Vampires in New England

New England was one of the first regions in North America to be colonized. Among the first settlers were the Puritans, passionate Protestants dedicated to stripping all Catholic vestiges from their faith and creating a "pure" new Christianity. Despite, or maybe because of, the early settlers' zeal, New England has always been vulnerable to superstitions and spiritual fads.

During the famous Salem witch trials of 1692, hundreds of men and women in Massachusetts were accused of witchcraft, and nineteen were convicted and hung. In the late nineteenth century, the spiritualism movement spread rapidly through the region. For a time, many New Englanders believed it was possible to communicate with the spirit world through séances—special meetings for consulting with the dead.

Consumption

Before modern medicine, a common cause of death in New England was tuberculosis, an infectious disease that primarily affects the lungs and can be fatal. Symptoms include weight loss, fever, and punishing, bloody coughs. When tubercular people cough or sneeze, they spread their bacterial infection through the air. Today, many Americans are protected against tuberculosis by immunization, and the active disease can be treated with antibiotics.

Consumption was a serious disease before the discovery of antibiotics. In this 1858 print by Henry Peach Robinson, a family watches a beloved daughter fade away.

Tuberculosis was once called "consumption" because the infected wasted away as if consumed from within. People didn't know what caused consumption, and they didn't know how to cure it, so they turned to traditional folk beliefs. In New England, when multiple people in one family died from consumption, the first person to die was believed to have become a vampire that returned from the grave to drain blood and vitality from his or her kin. History records the details of some of these creepy cases.

The Science of Vampires

Many scientists have attempted to find scientific explanations for the vampire legend. Author Nancy Garden and biochemist David Dolphin have both speculated that the rare genetic disease porphyria might have inspired many vampire stories. Some forms of porphyria can cause anemia (a low count of red blood cells, which leads to weakness and tiredness), sensitivity to light, and increased hair growth, among other symptoms. Porphyria is common in eastern Europe and could have become more common among the inbred nobility. Other conditions that scientists have suggested might explain vampire tales include catalepsy and rabies.

In his book *Vampires, Burial, and Death*, scholar Paul Barber attempts to explain eastern European vampire folklore by examining the natural process of decomposition. Barber points out that some corpses decay faster than others. A body laid to rest in the cold winter ground will remain better preserved than a body buried in high summer. Superstitious folk digging up a body buried in winter might have been surprised by how healthy it looked. A dead body's skin naturally recedes, creating the illusion that the teeth, nails, and hair have grown. But how can one explain reports of vampire corpses swollen with blood, with red cheeks and bloody mouths? Barber explains that after death, corpses swell with natural gases. The increased pressure inside the body can push blood out of the nose and mouth. The corpse then appears engorged with blood.

Sarah Tillinghast (Exeter, Rhode Island, 1799)

One of the earliest cases of vampirism in New England was not recorded in writing until a century later. However, the legend resonates with the folk beliefs that prevailed in the region at the time.

Rhode Island farmer Stukeley "Snuffy" Tillinghast had a large and happy family, boasting fourteen children in all. But tragedy struck when his oldest girl, Sarah, died of consumption. Soon after, six of her brothers and sisters followed. Snuffy's wife, Honor, complained that she was losing energy. She was also plagued by horrific dreams, in which Sarah came back from the grave to torment her.

The residents of Exeter decided to exhume the Tillinghast children. According to the story, when they opened Sarah's coffin, her body was suspiciously well preserved. They resorted to an old remedy against vampires: they removed Sarah's heart, and the hearts of her siblings, and burned them all. Then they reburied the bodies. One more Tillinghast child died, but the deaths stopped there.

Nancy Young (Foster, Rhode Island, 1827)

Nancy Young was just nineteen when she died of consumption. Her devastated father, Levi, grew even more disconsolate when several of her siblings lost their strength and began to fade from this mortal world. Levi had Nancy's remains exhumed and burned, and he directed his children to breathe in the ashes of their sister's vampirish corpse. Sadly, this last-ditch effort to save the family was in vain. Five more of Nancy's brothers and sisters passed away soon afterward.

Lemuel and Elisha Ray (Jewett City, Connecticut, 1854)

The Rays of Jewett City, Connecticut, a family of seven, were struck by a familiar disaster. Within the space of ten years, the family's father and two sons passed away. When a third son, named Henry Nelson, took sick, the community decided to take drastic measures. They raised the bodies of brothers Lemuel and Elisha Ray from their final resting places and put them to the torch. All was in vain: Henry Nelson died.

Mercy Brown (Exeter, Rhode Island, 1892)

Perhaps the most famous New England vampire story unfolded just before the dawn of the twentieth century. Mary E. Brown and George T. Brown had a large family in Exeter, Rhode Island. Tragically, in December 1883, Mary died of consumption. She was soon followed by her oldest daughter, Olive. Next, nineteen-year-old Mercy expired and Edwin, the family's oldest son, took sick. Desperate to save Edwin as he lingered on death's door, George Brown decided that one of his dearly departed could have become a vampire.

Mercy Brown's final resting place in Rhode Island continues to draw vampire enthusiasts and curiosity seekers, some of whom leave flowers and other offerings on her grave.

When their bodies were disinterred (dug up), Mary and Olive had already rotted away, but Mercy's body lay on its side in the coffin. She seemed barely decomposed, and her heart appeared to contain fresh liquid blood. (Mercy had been in the ground for only two months—and during the winter.) Mercy's heart and liver were removed from her body, placed on a rock (a common step in vampire executions), and burnt to a crisp. The family doctor recommended that Edwin drink the ashes as a medicine. Two months later, Edwin died.

Chapter 3

Vampires in the South

The South is a melting pot of supernatural beliefs. Of all the cities of the Old South, New Orleans has a particularly haunted history. Founded by the French, the city was also once ruled by the Spanish and has been influenced heavily by the Creoles (the descendents of French and Spanish colonials), African slaves, and Irish and German immigrants. The city has a unique spiritual profile, a rich gumbo of European, Native American, and African religious, spiritual, and superstitious folk beliefs.

Death in New Orleans

New Orleans has always approached death in a unique way. New Orleans's most famous cemeteries are below sea level. If bodies were buried in graves, after a storm water would soak the ground and send the coffins floating in the streets. So the city's dead are buried in aboveground tombs, making cemeteries look like miniature cities of the dead. The tomb of Marie Laveau, New Orleans's greatest "voodoo queen," or voodoo spiritual leader, is a tourist attraction that is always decorated with offerings, coins, and graffiti.

The city is also well known for its jazz funerals. A brass band leads a funeral procession to the church with a solemn dirge; on the way out of the

The crypt of famous voodoo priestess Marie Laveau is the highlight of many New Orleans cemetery and ghost tours. Visitors draw three Xs on the tomb in the hope that Laveau's spirit will grant them a wish.

church, it plays joyful, upbeat jazz as a way to begin the wake. Death just seems closer in New Orleans. Perhaps that's why so many famous vampire books, movies, and television series have been set in the Crescent City.

New Orleans is also home to vampire folk traditions. For instance, traditionally, when a member of a Louisiana family died, his relatives "sat up" with him, guarding the body until it was buried. Today, this is most often described as a way of showing respect and care for the deceased. However, the tradition is descended from European practices intended to make sure that the

New Orleans Voodoo and Hoodoo

New Orleans is home to two fascinating spiritual/magical practices: hoodoo and voodoo.

Hoodoo is a traditional form of African American folk magic that uses spells as well as charms made out of roots, minerals, candles, and other household and/or magical objects. Once widespread in the South, hoodoo's influence continues to be felt in New Orleans today.

New Orleans is also home to Louisiana voodoo. This religion has roots in vodun, an African religion brought to Louisiana in the eighteenth century by slaves from Benin. In the cultural crucible of New Orleans, vodun blended with Catholicism. Voodoo retained the belief in spirit and ancestor worship, but several vodun spirits and deities were fused, or combined, with Catholic saints. These spirits are contacted through ecstatic dance and singing, as well as snake handling.

A number of voodoo queens, including the famous Marie Laveau, presided over rituals in New Orleans and made amulets and other charms for followers. This practice overlapped with and influenced hoodoo. One local superstition says that if a woman puts a drop of her own blood in her husband's coffee, he will never leave her.

corpse showed no signs of becoming a vampire. If a dog growled at the body or a cat happened to stand on the coffin, the family would know to beware a visit from the undead.

The Legend of the Casket Girls

One of the most chilling vampire legends in this region is also one of the oldest. During New Orleans's early days as a French colony, the city was a rough-and-tumble place. Men vastly outnumbered women, and brides were in short supply. The women who did make it to the colony were often criminals or prostitutes.

So in the early 1700s, the French rulers of the colony brought over groups of young "good girls" to marry settlers. These young women were nicknamed "casket girls" because they brought their belongings and marriage trousseaus in wooden boxes called *cassettes*, which looked like caskets. The young women went to live in the French Quarter's old Ursuline convent until they selected a husband. In the meantime, the story says, the "caskets" were stored in the convent's attic.

The Ursuline convent in New Orleans is one of the oldest buildings in the Mississippi Valley. Note the shuttered attic windows.

According to local legend, these caskets contained vampires. People say that some of the caskets, with their resident vampires, are still stored inside the Ursuline convent's attic. Today, the convent supposedly has each of its upstairs windows fastened shut with screws blessed by the pope. These sealed windows sometimes mysteriously burst open in the night—and are immediately resealed.

Chapter 4

Vampires in the Southwest and Beyond

Most people associate vampires with wintry landscapes and haunted forests. But the vast deserts of the Southwest are home to their own uniquely American vampire lore.

The Southwest has always been heavily influenced by Native American culture, as well as the traditions of nearby Mexico and Central America. The Hopi and Navajo tell tales of the skinwalker, an evil, shape-shifting witch who can take the form of an animal. Supposedly, in order to gain this power, the skinwalker first learns the ways of witchcraft. Then it turns to the dark side, cementing its viciousness by killing a close relative. Skinwalkers are renowned for using human bones in charms, which are used to control their victims.

The Navajo belief in the skinwalker is so strong that many Navajos are reluctant to mention the term or to discuss it with nonnatives. As late as the mid-1970s, a lawyer sued a supposed skinwalker for tampering in a child custody case.

In Mexico, the Nahua people fear the *tlahuelpuchi*, a type of traditional witch that is born with a curse. According to popular superstitions, she has the

The lore, rituals, and beliefs of the Navajo are still a mystery to most outsiders. In this 1904 photograph, three Navajos named Tonenili, Tobadzischini, and Nayenezgani appear in ceremonial dress.

power to transform herself into various animals—the better to roam the night, sucking blood from babies' bodies.

The Curious Case of the Chupacabra

According to legend, the Southwest is home to another horrifying bloodsucking creature: the *chupacabra*, or "goat sucker." It earned this name because it attacks livestock, such as goats, and sucks their blood until their carcasses run dry.

The chupacabra is a cryptid, an animal whose existence has not been confirmed by science. The first North American chupacabra sighting occurred

Phylis Canion shows the head of an animal she holds responsible for killing chickens on her Texas ranch in 2007. She suspected the creature was a chupacabra, but researchers analyzing its DNA claimed it was a coyote with mange.

in 1956 in Arizona. But it wasn't until the 1990s that the chupacabra became a rising star in the world of vampiric creatures. In 1995 in Orocovis, Puerto Rico, a farmer found eight of his sheep lying dead and bloodless in the fields. The sheep did not appear to have been attacked by coyotes, dogs, or wolves: their bodies were in pristine condition except for a few puncture wounds on their necks.

It soon became apparent that a new type of creature was out for blood in Puerto Rico. The same year, cows, chickens, and people were attacked throughout the island. Many of the livestock appeared to have been killed by wounds to their necks. The town of Canóvanas was stunned when literally hundreds of area livestock were killed. The mayor, Jose Soto, became so concerned that he led the town in a chupacabra hunt. Residents used a goat as bait to lure the elusive vampire within shooting range. They never caught a chupacabra.

Vampire Bats

Northern Mexico and Latin America are home to an infamous—and very real—vampire: the vampire bat. Three bat species, found from northern Mexico to South America, exist on a gory diet: blood, and blood alone. They hunt at night, stealthily feeding upon sleeping animals. Using their fangs to make an incision in their prey, the bats lap up blood. Their fangs also inject saliva into the wound. This saliva contains a glycoprotein, aptly named draculin, that prevents the victims' blood from clotting while they feed.

Vampire bats live in the dark, founding colonies in caves, old temples, and hollow trees. Interestingly, vampire bats are very generous animals among themselves. They will adopt orphaned baby bats, and they are even known to feed starving bats by regurgitating blood from their own stomachs.

Chupacabra sightings spread across Puerto Rico and throughout the Caribbean, Central America, South America, and the southwestern United States. Today, people claim to have spotted chupacabras in such far-flung places as Maine, the Philippines, and Russia. In Florida, people blamed the chupacabra when sixty-nine goats, chickens, and ducks were found bloodless on a long, green lawn.

People involved in the earliest chupacabra sightings described the creature as reptilian, walking on two legs, with sharp spines down its back. Sometimes the creature was reported to have fangs or claws, or to be covered in gray hair. Other reports mentioned a long, snake-like tongue, burning and glowing red eyes, and a strong smell of sulfur. Some even said it had small wings.

However, as the chupacabra reports spread, the descriptions of the beast changed. The chupacabra was still described as a mysterious, bloodsucking beast preying upon innocent livestock. But now, it was said to run on four legs and look more like a mammal, as large as a small bear.

Scientific Explanations of the Chupacabra

According to a 2010 *National Geographic* article, in recent years, farmers have shot and killed animals they thought might be chupacabras and shared the carcasses with scientists. The scientists examining the bodies identified them as coyotes suffering from a painful disease called mange, which causes hair to fall out and skin to shrivel, as well as weakness and exhaustion. These coyotes probably preyed upon livestock because they were easier to hunt than wild animals.

However, some chupacabra enthusiasts reject the mangy coyote explanation, insisting that the chupacabra is an entirely different animal. There are even those who believe that chupacabras are alien pets or experiments that were brought to this planet on spaceships!

Chapter 5

Vampires in California: Hollywood's Famous Vampires

There is one region of the United States that has spawned hundreds of vampires: California, specifically Hollywood. By taking vampires off the page and putting them on the silver screen, Hollywood has spread vampire legends around the world.

Vampires in Literature

Since the nineteenth century, vampires have been popular subjects in literature. First, John Polidori, personal doctor to famous British poet Lord Byron, wrote *The Vampyre* (1819). It was based on a story by Lord Byron and starred an aristocratic and demonic vampire who reminded many people of, well, Lord Byron.

The serialized novel *Varney the Vampyre; Or, the Feast of Blood* was written in Britain in the mid-1840s as a series of cheap pamphlets known as penny dreadfuls. When the entire work was published, it included more than 220 chapters! Also in the 1840s, Edgar Allen Poe, the American master of the macabre, wrote several short stories about the dead returning from the

The director of the Dracula Museum in Alten-Buseck, Germany, gazes at a first edition of Bram Stoker's novel *Dracula*. *Dracula* was not the first vampire book, but it influenced all of the vampire tales that followed it.

grave to prey upon the living. The novel *Carmilla* by Irish author Joseph Sheridan Le Fanu, published in 1872, featured a mysterious but beautiful woman preying on a lovely girl.

But the vampire novel that truly captured the world's imagination was *Dracula* (1897) by Irish journalist, theater critic, and stage manager Bram Stoker. The character Dracula was the template of the classic Hollywood vampire: a haughty, imperious count who seduced his victims and then held them in his thrall.

Mexican Dracula

Few people realize that there is actually a Spanish-language version of the original 1931 film *Dracula*. In Hollywood at the time, it was common practice to shoot two different versions of a movie using the same sets and costumes. One version of the movie was shot during the day and another at night. The Spanish language *Dracula* stars different actors and is longer and more daring than the American *Dracula*. In fact, many viewers consider the Spanish version a far better film than the American vampire classic!

Since the publication of Stoker's novel, stage and screen adaptations have condensed, twisted, and transformed the original story. Still, the plot of *Dracula* is familiar to us today: lawyer Jonathan Harker travels to Castle Dracula in Transylvania on a business trip and meets the count himself. In the second half of the book, Dracula moves to London, where he fixates on Harker's fiancée, Mina, and her friend, Lucy. The count also earns a fan—a mental patient named Renfield who eats insects. He reveres Dracula as a master of sucking others' life force.

When Lucy wastes away, Professor Abraham van Helsing realizes she has become a vampire and stakes her through the heart. Next, Dracula feeds off Mina, and she, too, slowly falls under his spell. Luckily, Dr. Van Helsing, Harker, and their friends use the connection between Mina and Dracula to defeat the fiend. In the end, the entire group follows Dracula back to Transylvania, and they finally kill him.

The Birth of Film

Since the early days of silent film, vampires have stalked the silver screen. The 1896 French movie *Le Manoir du Diable* ("The Manor of the Devil") was just three minutes long. It featured a sorcerer who transforms into a giant bat.

Across the globe, movies based on vampires became popular. Successful films included *The Vampire* in 1910, the Italian *Tower of the Vampire* in 1913, the 1920 Russian *Dracula*, and the 1921 Hungarian *Drakula*.

One of the spookiest early vampire films was *Nosferatu* (1922) by German filmmaker F. W. Murnau. The film was a close adaptation of Stoker's novel *Dracula*, but the title and character names were changed to avoid copyright infringement. (Florence Stoker, the author's widow, sued the filmmaker anyway.) *Nosferatu* is an expressionistic movie, full of horrific images and

The movie *Nosferatu* (1922) was one of the first, and most terrifying, vampire movies. Above is the repulsive Count Orlok, played by Max Schreck.

dramatic special effects. Vampire Count Orlok is closely modeled on ancient folkloric vampires: he is bald, with a twisted face, disgustingly long fingernails, and fangs.

Of course, the most famous vampire movie is *Dracula* (1931). Based on the 1924 hit stage play, the movie was a "talkie," one of the earliest films with a sound track. The star of both the play and film—Hungarian actor Bela Lugosi—would become the most iconic Dracula in history. Lugosi, with his

In this still from the classic 1931 movie *Dracula*, directed by Tod Browning, Count Dracula, played by Bela Lugosi, menaces the sleeping Lucy Weston, portrayed by actress Frances Dade.

dark hair, sharp nose, long black cape, and thick accent, would forever be identified with the Transylvanian count.

The Evolution of the Vampire

Throughout the 1930s and 1940s, vampire movies were released nearly every year. At first, there were sequels and spin-offs and later on, spoofs, parodies, and send-ups. The vampire movies changed to reflect the hopes and fears of each new era.

In the mid-1950s, America was engaged in a space race with its rival, the Soviet Union. The national obsession with outer space was reflected in a crop of vampire science-fiction movies like *Not of This Earth* (1957), *It! The Vampire from Beyond Space* (1958), *First Man into Space* (1959), and the legendary cult classic *Plan 9 from Outer Space* (1959).

In the 1960s and 1970s, London's Hammer Studios made brightly colored, sensational, and shocking vampire movies that were full of blood and gore. Christopher Lee, the studio's regular Dracula, and Peter Cushing, as Van Helsing, became legendary. The pair starred in movies such as *Horror of Dracula* (1958), *The Brides of Dracula*

British actor Christopher Lee was one of the film industry's most iconic vampires. He played Count Dracula in many different horror films produced by London's Hammer Studios.

(1960), *Dracula: Prince of Darkness* (1966), *Dracula Has Risen from the Grave* (1968), and *Dracula A.D. 1972* (1972). Their work had a huge influence on the American work produced in Hollywood.

From 1966 to 1971, the first important vampire character appeared on television: Barnabas Collins, the vampire star of ABC's gothic soap opera *Dark Shadows*. Actor Jonathan Frid played the vampire.

The cultural trends of the 1980s were reflected in that decade's vampires. Rock star David Bowie costarred in goth classic *The Hunger* in 1983. Vampires even found their way into the celebrated teen movies of the 1980s: *The Lost Boys* (1987) presented a gang of teenage vampires living in California.

In the 1990s, Francis Ford Coppola brought Bram Stoker's original story to life in vivid images in *Bram Stoker's Dracula* (1992). In *Blade* (1998), Wesley Snipes played a half-vampire vampire hunter (based on a popular Marvel comic book character) working to make the world safe for humans. At the start of the new millennium, the action movie *Underworld* (2003) and its sequels were set in a dark world with vampires and werewolves battling for supremacy.

Chapter 6

Vampires in Pop Culture Today

Today, vampires enthrall audiences in books, movies, video games, TV, and even children's television. In this chapter, we'll look at a few of the most important vampires that shape our current culture.

Vampires, with their endless lives and ability to move through different times and places, are perfectly suited to long-form storytelling. Vampires have starred in novels in every genre, including fantasy, sci-fi, and romance. In addition, vampires have been at the heart of several blockbuster TV and film series.

Anne Rice's Vampire Books

Anne Rice's book *Interview with the Vampire* (1976) became the most popular and influential vampire book since *Dracula*. Its success led to a beloved series of more than twelve novels.

Anne Rice is a native of New Orleans, and her novels often linger in that city. Some of her vampires are globetrotters that have spent time in eastern Europe, England, France, ancient Egypt, Constantinople, Venice, San Francisco, Washington, D.C., and other locales. Rice's vampires are glamorous, artistic, and emotional, and they fall in love easily. Many traditional vampire rules don't apply to them. For instance, they can safely look at a cross, and they can't be killed with a stake through the heart. Some have magical powers. They do need to drink blood, however, and sunlight can kill those vampires who are still relatively young—say, less than a thousand years old.

So far, the Anne Rice books have spawned two movies: *Interview with the Vampire* (1994) with Tom Cruise, Brad Pitt, and Kirsten Dunst, and *The Queen of the Damned* (2002), starring Aaliyah.

Chelsea Quinn Yarbro's Saint-Germain Novels

Author Chelsea Quinn Yarbro created a series about an immortal vampire named Count Saint-Germain, based on a historical count rumored to be an alchemist. According to Jacques Casanova's memoirs, the count claimed to be three hundred years old.

In Yarbro's books, Saint-Germain is a vampire. The continuing series follows his adventures through history: he spends time in medieval Florence, ancient Rome, the Old West, Moorish Spain, and many other places. Saint-Germain is a good vampire who tries to use his powers to help people. Unlike other vampires, he prefers to take small amounts of blood from willing victims. Interestingly, Saint-Germain does not sleep in a coffin. In order to rest on native soil, he has special compartments built into his shoes and the foundations of his houses.

Buffy the Vampire Slayer

Vampires have played an important role in recent television shows and movies, as well as books. First, in the movie *Buffy the Vampire Slayer* (1992), a Southern California cheerleader learns that she has been chosen by fate to slay vampires. Following the movie's success, screenwriter and filmmaker Joss Whedon created the long-running TV series *Buffy the Vampire Slayer* starring Sarah Michelle Gellar. In turn, the show led to novelizations, comics, video games, and a popular spin-off TV series called *Angel*.

Sarah Michelle Gellar appears as Buffy, and David Boreanaz as Angel, in writer Joss Whedon's classic vampire TV series *Buffy the Vampire Slayer*.

The "Buffy-verse" is full of demons, robots, witches, warlocks, and other marvelous beings. It's a world with complex and nuanced storylines that sometimes spin out in different directions. There are few series that have had more devoted and active fans.

Charlaine Harris's Southern Vampire Series

The Southern Vampire Mysteries by Charlaine Harris are set in a world where vampires coexist with humans. In the first book, *Dead Until Dark* (2001), the invention of Japanese synthetic blood has made it possible for vampires to "come out of the coffin" and make their identities public. However, vampires face human prejudice—and some refuse to give up hunting. What's more, vampires are in danger because their blood has magical properties when ingested by humans.

In 2008, the book series was adapted into a hit HBO show for adults called *True Blood*, with Anna Paquin as psychic barmaid Sookie Stackhouse and Stephen Moyer as her vampire boyfriend, Bill Compton. As of 2011, the show had garnered numerous awards, including a Golden Globe and an Emmy.

Stephenie Meyer's *Twilight* Novels

The Twilight series is one of the most phenomenally successful young adult book series ever. In the first book, *Twilight* (2005), heroine Bella Swan moves from sunny Phoenix to perpetually foggy Forks, Washington, to live with her father. There, she meets and falls in love with an impossibly handsome vampire named Edward. Edward looks like a teenager, but he is actually 104 years old. He survives on animal, instead of human, blood. When another vampire threatens Bella, Edward and his family struggle to protect her. Sequels include *New Moon* (2006), *Eclipse* (2007), and *Breaking Dawn* (2008). Eventually, Bella faces a choice between Edward and close friend and rival love interest Jacob, who just happens to be a werewolf.

The success of the Twilight series of movies has made actors Kristen Stewart, who plays Bella Swan, and Robert Pattinson, who plays Edward Cullen, into huge movie stars.

The book series was adapted into several incredibly successful movies, starring Kristen Stewart and Robert Pattinson. The Twilight novels and movies have become so popular that the real-life town of Forks, Washington, is now a tourist destination.

L. J. Smith's Vampire Diaries

The latest series of vampire novels to spawn a hit TV show, L. J. Smith's Vampire Diaries series, tells the story of teen Elena Gilbert, who must choose between two vampire brothers competing for her affection. There are several related book series: the Return series, the Hunters series, and Stefan's Diaries.

In this still from the TV show *The Vampire Diaries*, Ian Somerhalder *(left)* appears as Damon, Nina Dobrev *(middle)* appears as Elena, and Paul Wesley *(right)* appears as Stefan.

In 2009, *The Vampire Diaries* became a TV series on the CW television network, starring Nina Dobrev, Paul Wesley, and Ian Somerhalder. It has already proved popular with teen audiences.

Video Games and More

Vampires have also infested the gaming world, in video games like the *Bloodrayne* series and the *Castlevania* series. For those who would rather play with dice than electronics, there are role-playing games like *Vampire: The Masquerade*, *Vampire: The Masquerade—Bloodlines*, and *Vampire: The Requiem*.

The Goth Subculture

The gothic novels of the Romantic Era were set in ruined medieval churches and graveyards, often featured vampires and ghosts, and revolved around dark secrets and morbid obsessions. Hundreds of years later, many of today's teens are drawn to this dark world. They express their interest in the dark, the morbid, and the supernatural by becoming "goths."

The first song in the music genre that came to be known as goth was Bauhaus's "Bela Lugosi's Dead" (1979). Bauhaus's fellow bands Siouxsie and the Banshees and the Damned also played moody post-punk and dressed in black with dramatic makeup. (However, none of these early bands actually called themselves goth.) Over the years, their fans forged a subculture inspired by gothic novels, horror movies, vampire lore, the occult, and the Victorian era. Later goth bands include Sisters of Mercy, Rosetta Stone, and Marilyn Manson.

Because goths are gloomy and fascinated with death, they are often misunderstood as advocating violence or satanism (devil worship). In reality, goths are usually tolerant, nonviolent, creative, and compassionate. They tend to favor black clothing, dark hair and makeup, punk gear including piercings, and medieval-inspired clothing elements like corsets and velvet skirts. Goths gravitate toward the literary works of Edgar Allen Poe, H. P. Lovecraft, and Anne Rice. Filmmaker Tim Burton has made many classic goth movies, including *Edward Scissorhands* and *The Nightmare Before Christmas*.

Many goths love vampires so much that they dress in Dracula-inspired gear, use makeup to make their skin paler, or even wear false vampire teeth!

Not even children are safe from vampires. In the Bunnicula books by James Howe, a family takes home a vampire bunny. The popular and long-running children's TV show *Sesame Street* features a Dracula-like character named the Count, who loves to—what else?—count. There is even a popular chocolate-flavored cereal called Count Chocula!

Conclusion

Over the years, vampires have undergone an incredible transformation. In centuries past, vampires were mindless corpses rotting in their graves that rose to suck the blood of the living. These vampires symbolized the forces we cannot control in nature.

Today's vampires are seductive, beautiful, and immortal. They are often loners who long to join human society but are exiled from it. Many are fundamentally good and struggle to suppress their lethal urges. They symbolize the forces we cannot control in ourselves.

Our vampires have gone from monsters to romantic heroes, from dead to immortal. Why?

In her book *Our Vampires, Ourselves*, Nina Auerbach theorizes that in every era of history, people create a new type of vampire to embody their hopes and fears. Maybe the same is true of every storyteller—including every novelist, TV producer, and movie director. For example, *Twilight* created a relationship between a girl and a vampire that demonstrates how teenage girls might both long for romance and still fear it.

How will our vampire stories develop in the future? Only one thing is certain: as society changes, our vampire legends will continue to evolve. Who knows? Perhaps one day we will discover our legends were based on real life all along.

Glossary

consumption An outdated name for pulmonary tuberculosis (TB). TB was once called consumption because victims looked as if they were being consumed, or eaten up, from the inside.

corpse A dead human body.

cryptid An animal that is widely rumored to exist, but whose existence has not been scientifically proven.

decomposition The process a dead plant, animal, or human undergoes as it is naturally broken down; the act of rotting.

engorged Swollen with blood.

epidemic An outbreak of a disease or condition that spreads rapidly and affects many different people in a population.

exhume To dig up or disinter a dead body from its grave.

expressionistic Having to do with a movement in the arts that emphasized expression of the artist's inner experiences.

iconic Characterized by fame; being a widely known symbol.

impale To pierce with a long and sharp stick, spear, pole, or stake.

imperious Having or showing arrogant assurance; domineering.

mange A skin disease caused by parasitic mites that is characterized by itching, hair loss, and inflammation.

occult Having to do with the supernatural, magical, or esoteric.

revenant Someone or something that returns from the dead.

superstition A belief or fear based on tradition or received knowledge, rather than science, reason, or experience.

trousseau The clothing, household linens, and other possessions collected by a bride for her marriage.

tuberculosis An infectious disease caused by bacteria. It often infects the lungs and can cause fever, weight loss, bloody coughs, difficulty breathing, fever, chest pain, and other symptoms.

For More Information

American Folklore Society
Mershon Center, The Ohio State University
1501 Neil Avenue
Columbus, OH 43201-2602
(614) 292-4715
Web site: http://www.afsnet.org
The American Folklore Society publishes a quarterly magazine and provides
    other resources for folklorists.

Haunted History Tours
97 Fountainebleau Drive
New Orleans, LA 70125
(504) 861-2727
Web site: http://www.hauntedhistorytours.com
Haunted History offers a number of tours of historic New Orleans, including
    a special vampire tour.

Le Musée des Vampires (The Vampire Museum)
14 rue Jules David
Les Lilas (93)
France
Web site: http://artclips.free.fr/musee_des_vampires/MuseeVampires1.html
This small, private museum near Paris is dedicated to the study of vampires and
    their place in folklore and culture. Tours are available by appointment only.

Museum of the Moving Image
36-01 35th Avenue
Astoria, NY 11106

(718) 784-0077
Web site: http://www.movingimage.us
The Museum of the Moving Image is dedicated to the history and art of moving pictures. It hosts exhibitions, screenings, and educational programs, in addition to offering research opportunities.

New Orleans Historic Voodoo Museum
724 Dumaine Street
New Orleans, LA 70116
(504) 680-0128
Web site: http://www.voodoomuseum.com
This small museum is dedicated to the history and culture of voodoo in New Orleans.

Transylvanian Society of Dracula (TSD)
Canadian Chapter
2309-397 Front Street W.
Toronto, ON M5V 3S1
Canada
Web site: http://www.blooferland.com/tsd.html
This international society is dedicated to the study of Dracula—both the fictional figure and the historical Vlad Tepes. In addition to hosting meetings and symposia, the organization offers special Transylvanian travel tours.

Web Sites

Due to the changing nature of Internet links, Rosen Publishing has developed an online list of Web sites related to the subject of this book. This site is updated regularly. Please use this link to access the list:

http://www.rosenlinks.com/amss/vamp

For Further Reading

Anderson, Jeffrey E. *Hoodoo, Voodoo, and Conjure: A Handbook.* Westport, CT: Greenwood Press, 2008.

Belanger, Jeff. *World's Most Haunted Places* (Haunted). New York, NY: Rosen Publishing, 2009.

D'Agostino, Thomas. *A History of Vampires in New England.* Charleston, SC: Haunted America, 2010.

Gee, Joshua. *Encyclopedia Horrifica: The Terrifying Truth About Vampires, Ghosts, Monsters, and More.* New York, NY: Scholastic, 2007.

Gideon, Amos, and Darren Zenko. *Native American Ghost Stories.* Auburn, WA: Lone Pine Publishing International, 2006.

Guiley, Rosemary. *The Encyclopedia of Vampires and Werewolves.* 2nd ed. New York, NY: Facts On File, 2011.

Guiley, Rosemary. *Vampires* (Mysteries, Legends, and Unexplained Phenomena). New York, NY: Chelsea House Publishers, 2008.

Hamilton, John. *Vampires* (The World of Horror). Edina, MN: ABDO, 2007.

Kallen, Stuart A. *Vampire History and Lore* (Vampire Library). San Diego, CA: ReferencePoint Press, 2011.

Krensky, Stephen. *Vampires* (Monster Chronicles). Minneapolis, MN: Lerner Publications, 2007.

Meyer, Stephenie. *Twilight.* New York, NY: Little, Brown and Company, 2005.

Pipe, Jim. *Vampires* (Tales of Horror). New York, NY: Bearport Publishing, 2007.

Robson, David. *Encounters with Vampires* (Vampire Library). San Diego, CA: ReferencePoint Press, 2011.

Shone, Rob. *Vampires: Legends of the Undead* (Graphic Tales of the Supernatural). New York, NY: Rosen Central, 2011.

Stoker, Bram, and Roger Luckhurst, ed. *Dracula* (Oxford World's Classics). New ed. Oxford: Oxford University Press, 2011.

Bibliography

Animal Planet. "Lost Tapes: Skinwalker, Navajo Shapeshifter: Animal Planet."
    2011. Retrieved April 9, 2011 (http://animal.discovery.com/tv/
    lost-tapes/skinwalker).

Auerbach, Nina. *Our Vampires, Ourselves*. Chicago, IL: University of
    Chicago Press, 1995.

Barber, Paul. *Vampires, Burial, and Death: Folklore and Reality*. New ed.
    New Haven, CT: Yale University Press, 2010.

Bell, Michael E. *Food for the Dead: On the Trail of New England's
    Vampires*. New York, NY: Carroll & Graf, 2001.

Bibeau, Paul. *Sundays with Vlad: From Pennsylvania to Transylvania, One
    Man's Quest to Live in the World of the Undead*. New York, NY: Three
    Rivers Press, 2007.

Carey, Bjorn. "El Chupacabra Mystery Definitively Solved, Expert Claims."
    LiveScience.com, March 23, 2011. Retrieved April 7, 2011 (http://
    www.foxnews.com/scitech/2011/03/23/el-chupacabra-mystery-
    definitively-solved-expert-claims).

Day, William Patrick. *Vampire Legends in Contemporary American Culture:
    What Becomes a Legend Most*. Lexington, KY: University Press of
    Kentucky, 2002.

Dresser, Norine. *American Vampires: Fans, Victims & Practitioners*. New
    York, NY: Norton, 1989.

FirstPeople.us. "Native American Legends: The Cannibal Who Was Burned:
    Haida." Retrieved April 7, 2011 (http://www.firstpeople.us/FP-Html-
    Legends/TheCannibalWhoWasBurned-Haida.html).

FirstPeople.us. "Native American Legends: How Mosquitoes Came to Be:
    Tlingit." Retrieved April 7, 2011 (http://www.firstpeople.us/FP-Html-
    Legends/How_Mosquitoes_Came_To_Be-Tlingit.html).

Herman, Marc. "Lost Tapes: The History of El Chupacabra: Animal Planet." Retrieved April 7, 2011 (http://animal.discovery.com/tv/lost-tapes/chupacabra/history).

Jenkins, Mark. *Vampire Forensics: Uncovering the Origins of an Enduring Legend.* Washington, DC: National Geographic, 2010.

Karg, Barbara, Arjean Spaite, and Rick Sutherland. *The Everything Vampire Book: From Vlad the Impaler to the Vampire Lestat—A History of Vampires in Literature, Film, and Legend.* Avon, MA: Adams Media, 2009.

Kelleher, Colm, and George Knapp. "Skinwalkers—What Are They?" Rense.com. Retrieved April 9, 2011 (http://www.rense.com/general77/skin.htm).

Library of Congress. "France in America: King's Daughters, Casket Girls, Prostitutes." Retrieved April 7, 2011 (http://international.loc.gov/intldl/fiahtml/fiatheme2b3.html).

MacDougal, Shane. *The Vampire Slayers' Field Guide to the Undead.* Huntingdon Valley, PA: Strider Nolan Publishing, 2003.

Maine Folklife Center, The University of Maine. "Northeast Folklore—Miscellaneous Malecite Tales." Retrieved April 7, 2011 (http://umaine.edu/folklife/publications/online-publications/northeast-folklore/miscellaneous-malecite-tales).

Melton, J. Gordon. *The Vampire Book: The Encyclopedia of the Undead.* 3rd ed. Canton, MI: Visible Ink Press, 2011.

Radford, Benjamin. *Tracking the Chupacabra: The Vampire Beast in Fact, Fiction, and Folklore.* Albuquerque, NM: University of New Mexico Press, 2011.

Taylor, Troy. "Haunted New Orleans History." 2000. Retrieved April 7, 2011 (http://www.prairieghosts.com/nohistory3.html).

Than, Ker. "Chupacabra Science: How Evolution Made a Mythical Monster." *National Geographic*, October 28, 2010. Retrieved April 7, 2011 (http://news.nationalgeographic.com/news/2010/10/101028-chupacabra-evolution-halloween-science-monsters-chupacabras-picture).

Index

About the Author

Sam Navarre is an educator in Brooklyn, New York. He has taught topics including acting, playwriting, art, current events, conflict resolution, and character education. Navarre has also penned many books for young adults on a variety of subjects. He and his wife, Rowena, are horror movie enthusiasts who have traveled to Transylvania several times.

Photo Credits